Every Animal Has a Home

by Mindy Menschell
illustrated by Tim Nihoff

Harcourt

Orlando   Boston   Dallas   Chicago   San Diego

Visit *The Learning Site!*

www.harcourtschool.com

Where do spiders live?

Spiders live on webs.
Here is a spider on its
web.

Where do bears live?

Bears live in dens.
Here is a bear in its den.

Where do birds live?

Birds live in nests.
Here is a bird in its nest.

Where do cows live?

Cows live in barns.
Here are some cows
in a barn.

Where do bees live?

Bees live in hives.
There are many
bees in a hive.

11

Every animal has a
home. Match each
animal with its home.